WITHDRAWN
from collection

WITHDRAWN
collection

D0184627

Moulton College

Class No, 636·737 BOR | R | C

Acc. No. T26238

Learning Resource Centre

the **Border Collie**

A guide to selection, care, nutrition,

upbringing, training, health, breeding,

sports and play.

Contents

Foreword

The book you are holding is a basic 'owners manual'
for everyone owning a Border Collie and also for those
who are considering buying a Border Collie. Too many
people buy a pet before really thinking about what
they're taking on, and our book is mainly intended to
give you the information you need to make a properly
considered decision before buying a Border Collie.

The golden rule is "think before you buy", and
this applies especially to the Border Collie.

The Border Collie has become enormously popular
over the past few years. This is hardly surprising, its
performance with sheep at the ever more popular she-
pdog trials is as impressive as its achievements
in agility competitions and other dog sports. It is
vital to preserve the Border Collie's excellent and
diverse characteristics in the breed, so it's important
to properly understand this very special dog.

This book will help you decide whether the Border
Collie is the right pet for you, and whether you in
turn can give this energetic dog what it needs.

Our book also goes into the broad history of the
Border Collie; it includes the breed standard and
will tell you what to look out for when buying a Border
Collie. It also contains information on feeding, upbringing and reproduction. Finally, it covers day-by-day
care, healthcare and some ailments typical of the breed.

If you want to know more about your favourite breed,
you can find an overview of some more literature on
the Border Collie at the end of this book.

We hope you enjoy reading about the Border Collie.

About Pets

A Publication of About Pets.

All rights reserved, including the right to
reproduce this book or portions
thereof in any form whatsoever.

Copyright © 2003
About Pets
co-publisher United Kingdom
Kingdom Books
PO9 5TL, England

ISBN 1852791810
First printing
September 2003

Original title: *de Border collie*
© 2001 - 2002 Welzo Media Productions bv,
About Pets bv,
Warffum, the Netherlands
http://www.aboutpets.info

Photos:
Ben Willemse, Marcelle Kauderer,
Rob Dekker, Piet Westelaken,
Tiny Goossens en
Suzan de Waal

Printed in Italy

In general

The name "Border Collie" can first be found in a 1570 publication by John Keys about English dog breeds, "De Canibus Britannicus". "Border", of course, takes us to the origin of the Border Collie – the Border Country, the border region between England and Scotland.

In this broad and rugged landscape, the breed became famous for its work with flocks of sheep. The origin and meaning of the word "Collie" are less certain and there are many theories. Some say it refers to the typical white "collar", while others believe it to be derived from "coaly", i.e. black. Another theory is that it goes back to the ancient Celts, who established themselves in the British Isles, and their Gaelic language in which "colley" means "useful".

Origin and history of the Border Collie

The fact that the wolf is the distant ancestor of all present-day dogs is easily recognised in the behaviour of a working Border Collie. The caution with which it approaches the flock, its careful creeping movements, its hypnosis of its prey with its eyes ("eye") are all typical of the hunting behaviour of the wolfpack. When two dogs are working together they naturally pick one side of the flock each.

A good working dog must, by nature, make use of its instincts, but must stop short of the final stage of the hunt, the conquest and devouring of its prey. Sheepdogs, from which today's Border Collie has gradually evolved, first appeared in England and Scotland during the 16th century. The contemporary Latin text mentioned above describes a type of medium-sized shepherd dog whose behaviour and working style were very similar to today's Border Collie. Responding to calls or whistles and even hand signals from its master, it would retrieve stray sheep and bring them back to the flock.

These dogs were indispensable helpers for this kind of job, as well as for treating and caring for individual animals. Without them some tasks would have been virtually impossible. The dogs were later bred specifically for this difficult work and a strict selection process was used. Their inherent guarding and herding abilities, but also their intelligence, obedience and endurance formed the most important criteria. Thus the Border Collie developed into a superb working dog, fast condemning the other British sheepdog breeds, such as the Bobtail and the Bearded Collie, to a life as family and show dogs. "Old Hemp", born in 1893, is

regarded as the direct forefather of the present-day Border Collie. He possessed outstanding talent, combined with a quiet and self-assured working manner, which won him respect and admiration. Farmers quickly realised that Hemp, with his controlled manner, was able to keep his flock under control and quiet, and this made him especially popular as a breeding dog. The first sheep herding competition, the equivalent of today's sheepdog trial, took place in 1873. Since then, these competitions, a test of ability where the best dogs are measured against their counterparts, have become ever more popular. They now also take place frequently in continental Europe, organised both by the kennel clubs and privately. The Border Collie is now found all over the world, and people everywhere have come to

cherish the talents of this special breed. Its nature, its manner of working, its intelligence and obedience together with its thoroughly loveable character and an enormous "will to please" naturally also appeal to people who don't need the Border as a working animal. And nowadays, more and more Border Collies are entrusted with other tasks than guarding sheep. They work as rescue dogs, guide dogs for the blind and other handicapped people or as search dogs seeking out drugs, explosives or disaster victims.

Border Collies have even been trained for security work or as sled dogs, and all this demonstrates just how flexible and adaptable the Border is. Whatever the task, it will always give 100% even when in difficulties or pain. Males almost never react to sexual stimuli when being worked. During trials, for example, they will concentrate totally on working the sheep, even when a bitch in season is close by.

Many have also discovered the Border Collie's talents as a sporting dog and, of course, the Border is unbeatable when it comes to obedience competitions or sports such as agility and flyball. It was inevitable that some breeders would eventually concentrate on breeding the Border Collie as a show dog. Most Border Collie owners that still use their dogs for their

original tasks, or who participate fanatically in sheepdog trials, look upon this with sadness. Many are convinced that most Border Collies bred from working strains cannot live without their sheep, and that all the sports mentioned above can never be a real alternative to demanding sheep work.

Character, the pros and cons of the Border Collie

After generations of being used only as a working dog, the Border Collie today is used and bred for many other purposes. Increasingly, even pure-bred Border Collies seem to possess no instinct for working with sheep. If you're looking for a quiet dog as good company, or if you don't want, or don't have the time, to let a Border Collie live a really active life, then you would be well advised to look for a different breed than a Border Collie. We've already talked about the outstanding qualities of the Border Collie; its special ability to guard and herd sheep (and other animals), its intelligence and its determination to please its master with its work. On top of these qualities come its toughness and a large measure of initiative. But however strange it may seem, in precisely these marvellous traits hide the disadvantages of the breed. The upbringing of a young Border demands knowledge and insight and, even more importantly, a calm and consistent approach. A Border Collie that is misunderstood and unable to work off his energy can develop serious behavioural problems. They are certainly not dogs for beginners. They're extremely clever and eager to learn, and they pick things up very quickly, the wrong things just as quickly as the right things. And once they've picked up bad habits, these can quickly become behaviour problems. A Border Collie needs a clever master with a quick mind who also enjoys lots of exercise. A walk in the woods or a run beside the bike won't satisfy its need to be worked and let off its energy. As well as plenty of opportunities to exercise, a Border Collie also needs mental challenges. Bottled-up energy needs to be released, and this can lead to destructive traits, aggression and straying. Its herding instinct can become directed at anything that moves: children as well as other dogs and pets such as cats. Cagebirds and rodents, even ants in procession must be hypnotised, circled and herded. This nervous, neurotic behaviour (which can't be corrected!) is not just a nuisance, but can easily become dangerous if it gets the chance to try to herd moving vehicles - cyclists, motorcyclists and cars. This has cost many a Border its life. The restlessness of many Border Collies can cause chronic eating disorders; they simply won't allow themselves the time to eat.

A frantic search for a tastier brand of food or forcing the dog to eat won't help at all. Regular feeds at fixed times in a quiet, closed room with no distractions are far more likely to succeed.

Just like the wolf's, the Border Collie's body talk is extremely expressive. Many display oversensitivity in response to their master's moods or to a raised voice with an immediate and ongoing show of subjection. They are constantly alert, they miss nothing and they react immediately, even to the tiniest non-verbal signal from their master. To an onlooker they appear to possess almost telepathic qualities.

Breed standard

A standard has been developed for all breeds recognised by the Kennel Club for the UK (and in Europe by the F.C.I. - the umbrella organisation for Western European kennel clubs). Officially approved kennel clubs in the member countries provide a translation. This standard provides a guideline for breeders and judges. It is something of an ideal, which dogs of the breed must strive to match.

Naturally, there is a connection between certain physical characteristics and performance, but for the Border Collie, which was bred for generations solely for its working qualities, appearance has long been of less significance. Until the British Kennel Club developed a standard for the breed in 1976, one was confronted with an enormous variety within the existing Border Collie population. This is why, in comparison to other breeds, a lot less has been established in terms of physique, coat and colouring characteristics. The official standard was only adopted by the F.C.I. in 1988.

The UK Border Collie Breed Standard

Character
The Border Collie must not appear nervous, nor may it be aggressive, but it should be lively, alert, quick to react and intelligent.

General appearance

The Border Collie should have a well proportioned appearance, its outline should be flowing and imply quality, grace and fine harmony, together with enough substance to give the impression that the dog is able to do its duty over long periods. Any tendency towards coarseness or weediness must be considered as undesirable.

Head and skull
The skull may be fairly wide without a pronounced bump on the rear head (occiput). Its cheeks should not be full or rounded. Its muzzle, tapering towards the nose, should be moderately short and strong. Skull and foreface are approximately equal in length. Its nose should be black, except on brown dogs when it may be brown. Nostrils should be well developed and the stop very distinct.

Eyes
The eyes should be set wide apart, oval-shaped and dark brown, except in Blue Merles where one or both, or part of one or both, may be blue. Its expression should be mild, keen, alert and intelligent.

Ears
The ears should be medium sized and moderately thick. They should be carried erect or semi-erect, set well apart and be sensitive in use.

Teeth and jaws
Teeth should be strong, perfect and form a complete scissor. The upper teeth should closely overlap the lower teeth, and the teeth should be set squarely in the jaws.

Neck
The neck should be of good length, strong and muscular but without exaggeration, and slightly arched and broadening towards the shoulders.

Forequarters
The front legs should be parallel when viewed from the front, the pasterns should appear slightly sloping when viewed from the side. The bone should be rounded and strong, but not heavy. Shoulders should be well laid back and elbows close to the body.

Body
The body should be athletic in appearance, ribs well sprung and

the chest deep and fairly broad, but not tucked up. The body should be slightly longer than the height at shoulders.

Hindquarters

The hindquarters should be broad and muscular, in profile sloping gracefully to set on the tail. Thighs should be long, deep and muscular with well arched knees and strong hocks, which should be placed low. The rear pasterns should have good bones and appear parallel when viewed from behind.

Feet

Oval in form, thick, strong and perfectly formed pads. Toes should be moderately arched and close together. Nails should be strong and short.

Gait

Movement should be free, smooth and tireless with minimum lift of feet, conveying the impression of the dog's ability to move with stealth and speed. Viewed from the front the dog should move straight, without signs of weakness in shoulders, elbows or wrists. Seen from the rear its legs drive it with power and grace, its hocks not too close together, but not too far apart.

Tail

The tail should be moderately long, the bone reaching at least to the hock. It should be set low,
well sprung with an upward swirl towards the end. The tail may be raised in excitement, but never carried over the dog's back.

Coat

The are two varieties of coat: The shorthaired and semi-long-haired. In both cases the topcoat should be weather resistant. The semi-long haired variety possesses superfluous hair on the neck, breech and tail. On the face, ears and forelegs (except for feather) and on the hind legs, hair should be short and smooth.

Colour

All possible colours are per-missible, but white should never predominate.

Size

Ideal height for dogs : 53 cm (21 inches), bitches slightly smaller.

Faults

Any deviation from the points above must be considered as a fault. The seriousness with which the fault should be regarded should be in proportion to the degree of deviation.

Note:

Males should have two clearly developed testicles, fully descended into the scrotum.

Breed standard by courtesy of the Kennel Club of Great Brittain

Buying a Border Collie

If, after careful consideration, you've decided to buy a Border Collie, there are a number of possibilities. Do you want a puppy or an adult dog? Should it be a male or female?

And, of course, the question arises as to where you should buy the dog. Should you buy it from privatly or from a reliable breeder? For your own and the animal's sake, a few things should be decided in advance. After all, you want a dog that fits your situation.

Male or female?

Whether you buy a male or a female is mainly a question of personal preference. Both can grow up to become attractive and well behaved members of the family. And as far as working capacity is concerned, there's no difference between dog and bitch.

Males sometimes seem somewhat more self-assured and can display dominant behaviour, trying to play the boss over other dogs, especial-

ly other males, and, if they get the chance, over humans too. In the wild the most dominant dog (or wolf) is always the leader of the pack. In many cases this is a male.

It is of the utmost importance for a good relationship between dog and master that the dog understands from the outset that you're the leader of the pack. This demands an understanding yet consistent upbringing. When females become fertile, usually between eight and twelve months, they go on heat. This happens twice per year and lasts two to three weeks. This is the fertile period when a female can mate and, especially during the second half of their season, they try to go out in search of a male. Measures need to be taken to prevent unwanted additions to the family. A male will display more masculine behaviour once he becomes sexually mature. He will make clear to other dogs which territory is his by urinating frequently and in as many places as possible. He's also difficult to keep in when there's a bitch in season in the area. As far as general care is concerned, there is little difference between male and female.

Puppy or adult dog?

After you've made the decision to buy a male or female, the next question rises. Should it be a puppy or a grown dog? Choosing a puppy is opting for a playful, energetic member of the family who can easily adapt to its new surroundings. Of course, it's great having a sweet pup in the house, and you have the best chance to influence its character and to bring it up. But the up-bringing of a young dog demands a lot of time. In the first year, it learns more than the rest of its life. Becoming house-trained, getting used to car journeys, walking on a lead and lots more. This is the period when the foundations for obedience and social behaviour are laid. You should recognise with the fact that, especially in the first few months, you will need to devote a lot of time to caring for your puppy, and bringing it up. If you do choose to buy a puppy, you need to find a breeder with a

litter. The popularity of the Border Collie has grown strongly over the past few years, and this means that a lot of puppies for sale have been bred purely for profit. Just how many puppies are for sale can be seen by the many advertisements, especially in the Saturday editions of newspapers. Some of these puppies will have a pedigree, but many won't. Their breeder will have paid no attention to possible breed-specific illnesses or in-breeding. The puppies were removed from their mother as fast as possible and missed the social training that she would give them in their early weeks. So never choose a puppy that is too young or whose mother you couldn't see. Incidentally, a pedigree is nothing more or less than a proof of descent. The kennel club also issues pedigree certificates for the young of parents that suffer from congenital defects, or that have never been checked for them. So a pedigree certificate says nothing about the health of the dog concerned.

On the other hand, you must realise that a pedigree is often essential if you want to participate with your dog in organised sports. Registration is also mandatory for entry into shows or for approved breeding with your Border.

The puppy service of the breeder clubs can help you with addresses for reliable breeders. The breed

federation exercises a very strict breeding policy intended to keep the Border Collie population healthy and free of congenital defects. It also allows its members to breed only with animals that:

• are registered with the Kennel Club or with a foreign sister organisation recognised by the Kennel Club.

• That have been declared by a vet

• authorised by the federation - as "definitely free" or "provisionally free" of any genetic eye diseases such as PRA, cataracts and Collie eye anomaly. Dogs to be used for breeding must be examined for

these ailments annually until they are six years of age. Only then can they be declared "definitely free" of these ailments.

You should preferably visit several breeders before actually buying your pup. Ask if the breeder is prepared to help you after your purchase and to find solutions with you for any problems that may come up.

Some breeders insist that by observing a litter and doing some tests they can select dogs with the desired character traits. Some also believe that one can test a six or seven week old puppy for its ability to work with sheep.

Things to watch out for

Buying a puppy is nothing to be sneezed at. You must look out for the following:

- Never buy a puppy on an impulse, even if it's love at first sight. A dog is a living being and needs a lot of care and attention. You choose a dog to be a comrade and companion for years.
- Never buy a puppy younger than eight weeks
- Take a good look at the mother. Is she quiet, nervous, aggressive, well looked after or neglected? The behaviour and appearance of the mother says a lot, not only about the breeder's quality, but also about the health of the puppy you're buying.
- Avoid buying a puppy whose mother was kept only in a kennel. A young dog needs as many impressions and experiences as possible during its early months, including family life. It can thus get used to humans, other pets and different sights and sounds. Kennel dogs miss these experiences and have not been

sufficiently socialised.

- Always ask to see the parent dogs' papers (vaccination certificates, pedigrees, official results of health checks, especially eye and HD examinations).
- Ask whether the pups have been vaccinated and wormed. Puppies must be vaccinated in the 6th, 9th and between the 12th and 14th week. Regular worming is also extremely important.
- If you're looking for a Border Collie to work with sheep, pick a puppy bred from working parents. Ask to see the mother and, if possible, the father at work, and ask about any tests of their herding behaviour and possible trials results.
- Don't be suspicious if this is the last puppy in the litter. Many puppies are chosen only for their external characteristics, and there are countless examples of so-called 'left-overs' developing into outstanding working dogs.
- Put any agreements with the breeder in writing.

Take such statements with a pinch of salt. A puppy test can give certain indications of its character, such as dominance or shyness. Learning of such characteristics at an early stage is naturally very useful. It can give you an advantage when bringing your dog up, but remember that any such test is only a snapshot. The environment it grows up in and its up-bringing also help to influence a puppy. Any interest in sheep may suddenly appear between its fifth and twelfth month. Even when buying an adult dog, it's worth getting in contact with the kennel club. They also help to place adult animals who can no longer be kept by their owner for various reasons (impulse buying,

moving, divorce). In this case try to get as much information as you can about the dog's background, and about its character, qualities and defects. This is extremely important if a Border Collie has to be moved because of behaviour problems. It will need a lot of knowledge and experience to help restore its balance and enable it to become a happy dog. This process can take as long as a year. When buying an adult Border Collie, you can ask whether you can have the dog for a few weeks on trial. Make clear agreements and put these in writing. Of course, the earlier remarks about registration and examination for hip problems and congenital eye disorders apply equally when buying an older Border Collie.

Two dogs?

Having two or more dogs in the house is not just nice for us, but also for the animals themselves. Dogs get a lot of pleasure from their own company. After all, they are pack animals. If you're sure that you want two young dogs, it's best not to buy them at the same time. Bringing a dog up and esta-blishing the bond between dog and master takes time and you need to give a lot of attention to the dog in this phase. Having two puppies in the house means you have to divide your attention. Apart from that, there's a chance that they will focus on one another rather than on their master. Buy the second pup when the first is (almost) an adult. Two adult dogs can happily be brought into the household together. Taking in a puppy when the first dog is somewhat older often has a positive effect on the older dog. The influence of the puppy seems almost to give it a second child-hood. The older dog, if it's been well brought up, can help with the up-bringing of the puppy. Young dogs like to imitate the behaviour of their elders. Don't forget to give both dogs the same amount of attention. Take the puppy out alone at least once per day during the first eighteen months. Ensure both dogs get enough peace and quiet. You have to force Border Collies to do this by separating them after a romp, because they never want to stop. The combination of a male and female needs special attention. If you don't plan to breed with your dogs, you must take measures to prevent them mating when the bitch is in season. Sterilisation of the female or castration of the male are possibilities, but the latter is usually only done on medical advice, or for behaviour reasons.

The Border Collie and children

Dogs and children are a great combination. They can play together and get great pleasure out of each other. Moreover children can learn to handle living beings. They develop respect and a sense of responsibility by caring for a dog, or other pets. Let children help look after the dog as much as possible. This will create a real bond. However sweet a dog is, children must understand that a dog is a living being and not a toy.

A dog isn't comfortable when it's messed around with. It can become frightened, timid and even aggressive. So make it clear what a dog likes and what it doesn't. Teach the child how it can play with the dog. Perhaps a game of hide and seek where the child hides and the dog has to find it. Even a simple tennis ball can give enormous pleasure. But you must recognise the fact that some Border Collies are fanatical game players and, as well as the ball or other toy, may sometimes snap at a hand. They can also jump high

and hard in their over-enthusiasm, and you must then really try to calm the dog down. Children must learn to leave a dog in peace when it doesn't want to play any more.

A young Border Collie with its limitless energy often won't know when to stop, and you must usually pick the moment when the game is over. A cage or an indoor kennel can be useful here, because a dog needs regular periods of rest for its growth. The arrival of a baby also means changes for the life of a dog. Before the birth you can help get the dog acquainted with the new situation. Let it sniff at the new things in the house and it will quickly accept them. When the baby has arrived involve the dog as much as possible in day-by-day events, but make sure it gets plenty of attention too.

NEVER leave a dog alone with young children. Crawling infants sometimes make unexpected movements, which can easily frighten a dog. And infants are hugely curious, and may try to find out whether the tail is fastened to the dog, or whether it can get its eyes out, just like they do with their cuddly toys. But a dog is a dog and it will defend itself when it feels threatened.

Travelling

Travelling with a dog is not always pure pleasure. Some dogs love a ride in the car while others need huge efforts to even get them in it.

Some dogs suffer from car-sickness their whole life. If you're planning a holiday in far-away places and want to take your dog with you, you should ask yourself whether you're really doing it a favour.

That very first trip

The first trip of a puppy's life is also the most nerve-wracking. This is the trip from the breeder's to its new home. If possible, pick up your puppy in the morning. It then has the whole day to get used to the new situation. Ask the breeder not to feed it that day. The young animal will be flooded with all kinds of new experiences. Firstly, it's away from its mother, brothers and sisters; it's in a small room (the car) with all its new smells, noises and strange people. So there's a high risk that the

puppy will be car-sick this first time, with the annoying consequence that it will remember riding in the car as an unpleasant experience.

So it's important to make this first trip as pleasant as possible. When picking up a puppy, always take someone with you who can sit in the back seat with the puppy on his lap and talk to it calmly. If it's too warm for the puppy a place on the floor at the feet of your companion is ideal. The pup will lie there relatively quietly and may even take a nap. Ask the breeder for a cloth or something else from the puppies basket or bed that carries a familiar scent. The puppy can lie on this in the car, and it will also help if it feels lonely during the first nights at home.

If the trip home is a long one, then stop for a break once in a while. Let your puppy roam and sniff around (on the lead!), offer it a little drink and, if necessary, do its business. And take care to lay an old towel in the car. It can happen that the puppy, in its nervousness, may urinate or be sick. It's also good advice to give a puppy positive experiences with car journeys. Make short trips to nice places where you can walk and play with it. A dog that doesn't like the car can be very problematic.

Taking your Border Collie on holiday

When making holiday plans, you also need to think about what you

are going to do with your dog during that time. Are you taking it with you, putting it into kennels or leaving it with friends? In any event there are a number of things you need to do in good time. If you want to take your dog with you, you need to be sure that it will be welcome at your holiday home, and what rules there are. If you're going abroad it will need certain vaccinations and a health certificate, which normally need to be done four weeks in advance. You must also be sure that you've made all the arrangements necessary to bring your dog back home to the UK, without it needing to go into quarantine under the rabies regulations. Your vet can

give you the most recent information. If your trip is to southern Europe, ask for a treatment against tics (you can read more about this in the chapter on parasites). Although dog-owners usually enjoy taking their dog on holiday, you must ask yourself whether the dog enjoys it too. Some dogs are very uncomfortable in a hot country. Days spent travelling in a car are equally unpleasant for many dogs, and as we already saw, some dogs suffer badly from car-sickness. There

are good medicines for this, but they can also have side-effects and it's questionable whether you are acting in your dogs best interests by insisting on taking it with you. If you do decide to take it, plan your holiday around it. Be sure that your holiday home offers enough opportunities for your dog to run. A lake or other water can offer a cool-off for an overheated dog and most Borders love swimming. Make regular stops at safe places during your journey, so that your dog can have

a good run. Take plenty of fresh drinking water with you, as well as the food your dog is used to. Don't leave your dog in the car when the sun is shining. The temperature can climb fast and this can be an awful and life-threatening situation for your dog. If you can't avoid it, park the car in the shade as far as possible and leave a window open for a little fresh air. Even if you've taken these precautions, never stay away longer than is strictly necessary.

If you're travelling by plane or ship, make sure in good time that your dog can travel with you and what rules you need to observe. You will need time to make all the arrangements. Maybe you will decide not to take your dog and you must then find somewhere for it to stay. Arrangements for a place in kennels need to be made well in advance, and there may be certain vaccinations required, which need to be done a minimum of one month before the stay.

If your dog can't be accommodated in the homes of relatives or friends, it might be possible to have an acquaintance stay in your house. This also needs to be arranged well in advance, as it may be difficult to find someone to look after your dog.

Always ensure that your dog can be traced should it run away or get lost while on holiday. A little

tube with your address or a tag with home and holiday address can avoid a lot of problems.

Moving home

Dogs generally become more attached to humans than to the house they live in. Moving home is usually not a problem for them. But it can be useful before moving to let the dog get to know its new home and the area around it. If you can, leave your dog with relatives or friends (or kennels) on the day of the move. The chance of it running away or getting lost is then practically zero. When your move is complete, you can pick your dog up and let it quietly get familiar with its new home and environment. Give it its own place in the house at once and it will quickly adapt. During the first week or so, always walk your dog on a lead, because an animal can also get lost in new surroundings. Always take a different route so it quickly gets to know the neighbourhood. Don't forget to get your new address and phone number engraved on the dog's tag. Send a change of address notice to the institution that has the chip or tattoo data.

Don't forget to get your new address and phone number engraved on the dog's tag. Send a change of address notice to the chip or tattoo registration office. Dogs must sometimes be registered in a new community.

Feeding your Border Collie

A dog will actually eat a lot more than just meat. In the wild it would eat its prey complete with skin and fur, including the bones, stomach and innards with its semi-digested vegetable material.

In this way the dog supplements its meat menu with the vitamins and minerals it needs. This is also the basis for feeding a domestic dog.

Ready-made foods

It's not easy to put together a complete menu for a dog yourself that includes all the necessary proteins, fats, vitamins and minerals in just the right proportions and quantities. Meat alone is certainly not a complete meal for a dog. It contains too little calcium. A calcium deficiency over time will lead to bone defects, and for a fast-growing puppy this can lead to serious skeletal deformities.

If you mix its food yourself, you can easily give your dog too much in terms of vitamins and minerals. This can also be bad for your dog's health. You can avoid these problems by giving it ready-made food of a good brand. These products are well-balanced and contain everything your dog needs. Supplements such as vitamin preparations are superfluous. The amount of food your dog needs depends on its weight and activity level. You can find guidelines on the packaging. Split the food into two meals per day if possible and always ensure there's a dish of fresh drinking water next to its food.

Give your dog the time to digest its food, don't let it outside straight after a meal. A dog should also never play on a full stomach. This can cause stomach torsion, where the stomach turns over, and this can be fatal for your dog.

Working Border Collies are only fed in the evenings after the work is done. Because the nutritional needs of a dog depend on its age and way of life, there are many different types of dog food available. There are "light" foods for less active dogs, "energy" foods for working dogs and "senior" foods for the older dog.

Dry puppy food

There is a wide range of dry puppy foods on the market these days. These foods have a higher content of substances that promote growth, as well as protein and calcium. Growing too fast, however, can also promote ailments such as hip and elbow dysplasia (see the chapter on Your Border Collie's health). So between the fourth and fifth month, switch to a lower energy food.

Canned foods, mixer and dry foods

Ready-made foods available at pet shops or in the supermarket can roughly be split into canned food, mixer and dry food. Whichever form you choose, ensure that it's a complete food with all the necessary ingredients. You can see this on the packaging. Most dogs love canned food. Although the better brands are composed well, they do have one disadvantage: they are soft. A dog fed only on canned food will sooner or later have problems with its teeth (plaque, paradontosis). Besides canned food,

give your dog hard foods at certain times or a dog chew. Mixer is a food consisting of chunks, dried vegetables and grains. Almost all moisture has been extracted. The advantages of mixer are that it is light and keeps well. You add a certain amount of water and the meal is ready. A disadvantage is that it must definitely not be fed without water. Without the extra fluid, mixer will absorb the fluids present in the stomach, with serious results. Should your dog manage to get at the bag and enjoy its contents, you must immediately give it plenty to drink.

Dry chunks have also had the moisture extracted but not as much as mixer. The advantage of dry foods is that they are hard, forcing the dog to use its jaws, removing plaque and massaging the gums.

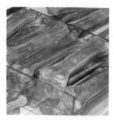

Dog chew products

Naturally, once in a while you want to spoil your dog with something extra. Don't give it blocks of cheese or sausage as these contain too much salt and fat. There are various products available that a dog will find delicious and which are also healthy, especially for its teeth, such as Nylabone. You'll find a large range in the pet shop.

The butcher's left-overs

The bones of slaughtered animals have traditionally been given to the dog, and dogs are crazy about them but they are not without risks. Pork and poultry bones are too weak. They can splinter and cause serious injury to the intestines. Beef bones are more suitable, but they must first be cooked to kill off dangerous bacteria. Pet shops carry a range of smoked, cooked and dried abattoir residue, such as pigs' ears, bull penis, tripe sticks, oxtails, gullet, dried muscle meat, and hoof chews.

Buffalo or cowhide chews

Dog chews are mostly made of beef or buffalo hide. Chews are usually knotted or pressed hide and can come in the form of little shoes, twisted sticks, lollies, balls and various other shapes; nice to look at and a nice change.

Munchy sticks

Munchy sticks are green, yellow, red or brown coloured sticks of various thickness. They consist of ground buffalo hide with a number of undefined additives. Dogs usually love them because these sticks have been dipped in the blood of slaughtered animals. The composition and quality of these between-meal treats is not always clear. Some are fine, but there have also been sticks found to contain high levels of cardboard and even paint residues. Choose a product with are clearly described ingredients.

Overweight?

Recent investigations have shown

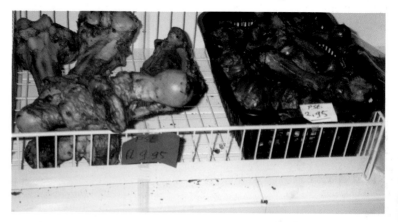

that many dogs are overweight. A dog usually gets too fat because of over-feeding and lack of exercise. Use of medicines or a disease is rarely the cause. Dogs that get too fat are often given too much food or to many treats between meals. Gluttony or boredom can also be a cause, and a dog often puts on weight following castration or sterilisation. Due to changes in hormone levels it becomes less active and consumes less energy. Finally, simply too little exercise alone can lead to a dog becoming overweight. You can use the following rule of thumb to check whether your dog is overweight: you should be able to feel its ribs, but not see them. If you can't feel its ribs then your dog is much too fat.

Overweight dogs live a passive life, they play too little and tire quickly. They also suffer from all kinds of medical problems (problems in joints and heart conditions). They usually die younger too. So it's important to make sure your dog doesn't get too fat. Always follow the guidelines on food packaging. Adapt them if your dog is less active or gets lots of snacks. Try to make sure your dog gets plenty of exercise by playing and running with it a lot. If your dog starts to show signs of putting on weight you can switch to a low-calorie food. If it's really too fat and reducing its food quantity doesn't help, then a special diet is the only solution.

Fresh meat

Should you want to give your dog fresh meat occasionally, never give it raw, but always boiled or roasted. Raw (or not fully cooked) pork or chicken can contain life-threatening bacteria. Chicken can be contaminated by the notorious salmonella bacteria, while pork can carry the Aujeszky virus. This disease is incurable and will quickly lead to the death of your pet.

Caring for your Border Collie

Good daily care is extremely important for your dog. A well-cared for dog is less likely to become ill. Caring for your dog is not only necessary but also a pleasure.

Master and dog are both getting attention, and it's an excellent opportunity for a game and a cuddle.

The coat

Caring for your dog's coat involves regular brushing and combing, together with checking for parasites such as fleas. How often a dog needs to be brushed and combed depends on the length of its coat. Border Collies are less demanding in this respect. The shorthaired variety needs very little maintenance outside the moulting season. The semi-longhaired Border may suffer from knotted hair, especially in the wet autumn and winter periods, which is best cut out with scissors. Use the right equipment for taking care of the coat. Combs should not be too sharp and you should use a rubber or natural hair brush. Always comb from the head back towards the tail, following the direction of the hair. If you get a puppy used to being brushed from an early age, it will enjoy having its coat cared for. Only bath a dog when it's really necessary. A Border Collie should never need washing, but should your dog have managed to enjoy a wonderful roll in a cow-pat, then it's time for a good scrub. Use a special dog shampoo and make sure it doesn't get into the dog's eyes or ears. Rinse the suds out thoroughly and only let it out again when it's properly dry, as shampoo removes fat from the skin and coat, and dogs can get colds too! A vet can prescribe special medicinal shampoos for some skin conditions. Always follow the instructions to the letter. Good flea prevention is highly important to avoid skin and coat problems. Fleas must be treated not only on the dog itself but also in its surroundings (see the chapter on parasites). Coat problems can also occur due to an allergy to certain food substances. In such cases, a vet can prescribe a hypo-allergenic diet.

Teeth

A dog must be able to eat properly to stay in good condition, so it needs healthy teeth. Check its teeth regularly. If you suspect that all is not well get in touch with your vet. Regular feeds of hard dry food can help keep your dogs teeth clean and healthy. There are special dog chews, such as Nylabone, on the market that help prevent plaque and help keep the animal's breath fresh. You can use

special toothbrushes for dogs, but a finger wrapped in a small piece of gauze will also do the job. Get your dog used to having its teeth cleaned at an early age and you won't have problems.

You can even teach an older dog to have its teeth cleaned. With a dog chew as a reward it will soon get used to it.

Nails

On a dog that regularly walks on hard surfaces, its nails usually grind themselves down. In this case there's no need to clip their nails. But it wouldn't do any harm to check their length now and again, especially with an older Border Collie, which has less exercise. Using a piece of paper, you can easily see whether its

nails are too long. If you can push the paper between the nail and the ground when the dog is standing, then the nail is the right length. Nails that are too long can bother a dog. It can injure itself when scratching, so they must be kept trimmed. You can buy special nail clippers in pet shops. Be careful not to clip back too far as you could damage the skin around the nail, which can bleed unpleasantly. If you feel unsure, have this necessary task done by a vet or an animal beauty parlour.

Special attention is needed for the dewclaw, this being the nail on the inside of the hind leg. Clip this

nail back regularly, otherwise it can get caught on it and become damaged. Your vet can remove this nail.

Eyes

A dog's eyes should be cleaned regularly. Discharge gets into the corners of the eye. You can easily remove them by wiping them downward with your thumb. If you don't like doing that, use a piece of tissue or toilet paper.

Keeping your dog's eyes clean will take only a few seconds a day, so do it every day. If the discharge becomes yellow this could point to an irritation or infection. Eye drops (from your vet) will quickly solve this problem.

Ears

The ears are often forgotten when caring for dogs. But they must be checked at least once a week. If its ears are very dirty or have too much wax, you must clean them. This should be done preferably with a clean cotton cloth, moistened with lukewarm water or baby oil. Cotton wool is not suitable due to the fluff it can leave behind. NEVER enter the ear canal with an object. If you neglect cleaning your dog's ears there's a substantial risk of infection. A dog that is constantly scratching at its ears might be suffering from dirty ears, an ear infection or ear mites. This makes a visit to the vet essential.

Bringing up your Border Collie

It is very important that your dog is properly brought up and is obedient. Not only will this bring you more pleasure, but it's nicer for your environment.

A pup can learn through playing what he may and may not do. Rewards and consistency are important tools in bringing up a dog. Reward it with your voice, a stroke or something tasty and it will quickly learn to obey. A puppy-training course can help you along the way.

(Dis)obedience

A dog that won't obey you is not just a problem for you, but also for your surroundings. It's therefore important to avoid unwanted behaviour. In fact, this is what training your dog is all about, so get started early. 'Start 'em young!' applies to dogs too. An untrained dog is not just a nuisance, but can also cause dangerous situations, running into the road, chasing joggers or jumping at

people. A dog must be trained out of this undesirable behaviour as quickly as possible. The longer you let it go on, the more difficult it will become to correct it. The best thing to do is to attend a special obedience course. This can help to correct the dog's behaviour, as well as helping the owner learns how to handle undesirable behaviour at home. A dog must not only obey its boss during training, but everywhere and at any time. You must always be consistent when training good behaviour and correcting annoying behaviour. Reward for good behaviour and never punish it after it obeys. If your dog finally comes after you've been calling it a long time, then reward it. If you're angry because you had to wait so long, it may feel it's actually being

punished for coming. It will probably not obey at all the next time for fear of punishment.

Try to take no notice of undesirable behaviour. Your dog will perceive your reaction (even a negative one) as a reward for this behaviour. If you need to correct the dog, then do this immediately. Use your voice or grip it by the scruff of its neck and push it to the ground. This is the way a mother dog calls her pups to order. Rewards for good behaviour are, by far, preferable to punishment; they always get a better result.

House-training

The very first training (and one of the most important) that a dog needs is house-training. The basis for good house-training is keeping a good eye on your puppy. If you pay attention, you will notice that it always sniffs or does turns around the same place before doing its business there. Pick it up gently and place it outside, always at the same place. Reward it abundantly if it does its business there. Always put a puppy out at the same times: mornings as soon as it's awake, before and after meals, every time it's been asleep or has been playing, and in the evenings before bedtime. It will quickly learn the meaning, especially if its rewarded with a dog biscuit for a successful attempt. It's not always possible to go out after every

snack or snooze. Lay newspapers at different spots in the house. Whenever the pup needs to do its business, place it on a newspaper. After some time it will start to look for a place itself. Then start to reduce the number of newspapers until there is just one left, at the front or back door. The puppy will learn to go to the door if it needs to relieve itself. Then you put it on the lead and go out with it. Finally you can remove the last newspaper. Your puppy is now house-trained. One thing that certainly won't work is punishing an accident after the event. A dog whose nose is rubbed in its urine or its droppings won't understand that at all. It will only get frightened of you. Rewarding works much better than punishment. An indoor kennel or cage can be a good tool to help in house-training. A puppy won't foul its own spot, so a kennel can be a good solution for the night, or during periods in the day when you can't watch it. But a kennel must not become a prison where the dog is locked up day and night.

First exercises

Obedience training for a Border Collie is actually a piece of cake. After all, a Border is intelligent, eager to learn and possesses a strong will to please its master. But to get the right result it is important to be clear and consistent during training. Commands should be short and clear, like 'Lie down!' or 'Stay there!'. Commands should always be in the same tone and must be clearly different from one-another. This also applies to any whistle commands you may want to teach your dog. Whistle commands are usually used when working and during sheepdog trials, where the dog is often a good distance away, sometime hundreds of metres, from his master. Be consistent once you have chosen the commands. If you want the dog to lie down, it's no use using 'Lie down!' once and 'Lay!' the next time. Once the dog has understood the intention, it should only be necessary to call a command once, clearly and in a certain tone.

Repeating a command actually makes your dog disobedient. If it doesn't react immediately, make a disapproving sound while walking towards it. Shouting usually doesn't have the desired result. Dogs have exceptional hearing, much better than a human's. Commands should be called in a quiet and preferably soft tone. Keep raising your voice for exceptional situations.

The basic commands for an obedient dog are those for sit, lie down, come and stay. But a puppy should first learn its name. Use it as much as possible from the first day on followed by a friendly 'Here'. Reward it with your voice and a stroke when it comes to

you. Your puppy will quickly recognise the intention and has now learned its first command in a playful manner. Don't appear too strict towards a young puppy, and don't always punish it immediately if it doesn't always react in the right way. When you call your puppy to you in this way have it come right to you. You can teach a pup to sit by holding a piece of dog biscuit above his nose and then slowly moving it backwards. The puppy's head will also move backwards until its hind legs slowly go down. At that moment you say 'Sit!' Use your free hand to gently push the hindquarters down. After a few attempts, it will quickly know this nice game. Use the 'Sit!' command before you

give your dog its food, put it on the lead or before it's allowed to cross the street.

Teaching the command to get the dog to lie down is similar. Instead of moving the piece of dog biscuit backwards, move it down vertically until your hand reaches the ground and then forwards. The dog will also move its forepaws forwards and lie down on its own. Again, help it with your free hand. Then say 'Lie down!' or 'Lay!' Lying down is useful when you want a dog to be quiet.

A dog learns to stay from the sitting or lying position. While its sitting or lying down, you call the command: 'Stay!' and then step back one step. If the dog moves with you, quietly put it back in position, without displaying anger. If you do react angrily, you're actually punishing it for coming, and you'll only confuse your dog. It can't understand that coming is rewarded one time, and punished another. Once the dog stays nicely reward it abundantly. Don't let it lay more than a few seconds in the beginning. Once it understands what's expected, you can make the time longer, and increase the distance between you and the dog at the same time. The stay command is useful, for example, when getting out of the car. A Border Collie that has mastered these basic commands can start to get acquainted with sheep at seven or eight months. The kennel club can give you information where you can further explore your Border's talents in that direction with expert guidance.

Courses
Obedience courses to help you bring up your dog are available across the country. These courses are not just informative, but also fun for dog and master.
With a puppy, you can begin with a puppy course. This is designed to provide the basic training. A puppy that has attended such a course has learned about all kinds of things that will confront it in later life: other dogs, humans, traffic and what these mean. The puppy will also learn obedience

and to follow a number of basic commands. Apart from all that, attention will be given to important subjects such as brushing, being alone, riding in a car, and doing its business in the right places. The next step after a puppy course is a young dog's course. This course repeats the basic exercises and ensures that the growing dog doesn't get into bad habits. After this, the dog can move on to an obedience course for full-grown dogs. For more information on where to find courses in your area, contact your local kennel club. You can get the address from the Kennel Club of Great Britain in London. In some areas the RSPCA organises obedience classes. Your local branch may be able to give you information.

Play and toys
There are various ways to play with your dog, You can romp and run with it, but also play a number of games, such as retrieving, tug-of-war, hide-and-seek and catching. Border Collies love this kind of game. A tennis ball is ideal for retrieving, you can play tug-of-war with an old sock or a special tugging rope. Play tug-of-war only when your dog has reached a year old. A puppy must first get its second teeth and then they need several months to strengthen. If you start too young, there's a real chance of your dog's teeth becoming deformed. You can use almost anything for a game of

hide-and-seek. A frisbee is ideal for catching games. Never use too small a ball for games. It can easily get lodged into the dog's throat.

Play is extremely important. Not only does it strengthen the bond between dog and master, but it's also healthy for both. Make sure that you're the one that ends the game. Only stop when the dog has brought back the ball or frisbee, and make sure you always win the tug-of-war. This confirms your dominant position in the hierarchy. Use the toys only during play so that the dog doesn't forget their significance. When choosing a special dog toy, remember that

dogs are hardly careful with them. So always buy toys of good quality that a dog can't easily destroy.

Be very careful with sticks and twigs. The latter, particularly, can easily splinter. A splinter of wood in your dog's throat or intestines can cause awful problems. Throwing sticks or twigs can also be dangerous. If they stick into the ground a dog can easily run into them with open mouth.

If you would like to do more than just play games, you can now also play sports with your dog. For people who don't get the opportunity to teach their dog to work with sheep, there are various other sporting alternatives such as fly-ball, agility and obedience. They offer your Border the opportunity to run off its boundless energy and satisfy its urge to perform.

Aggressiveness

Border Collies are absolutely not aggressive by nature. Indeed, if they're properly socialised as a puppy and not subjected to bad experiences with humans, they will generally be friendly and trustful, even towards strangers. But every dog-owner should understand the background of aggression in dogs. You might have to be able to deal with it.

There are two different types of aggressive behaviour: The anxi-ous-aggressive dog and the domi-nant-aggressive dog. An anxious-aggressive dog can be recognised by its pulled back ears and its low position. It will have pulled in its lips, showing its teeth. This dog is aggressive because it's very frigh-tened and feels cornered. It would prefer to run away, but if it can't then it will bite to defend itself. It will grab its victim anywhere it can. The attack is usually brief and, as soon as the dog can see a way to escape, it's gone. In a con-frontation with other dogs, it will normally turn out to be the loser. It can become even more aggres-sive once it's realised that people or other dogs are afraid of it. This behaviour cannot be corrected just like that. First you have to try and

understand what the dog is afraid of. Professional advice is a good idea here. The wrong approach can easily make the problem worse.

The dominant-aggressive dog's body lanquage is different. Its ears stand up and its tail is raised and stiff. This dog will always go for its victim's arms, legs or throat. It is extremely self-assured and highly placed in the dog hierarchy. Its attack is a display of power rather than as a consequence of fear. This dog needs to know who's boss. You must bring it up rigorously and with a strong hand. An obedience course can help.

A dog may also bite itself when in pain. This is a natural defensive reaction. In this case try to resolve the dog's fear as far as possible. Reward him for letting you get to the painful spot. Be careful, because a dog in pain may also bite its master! Muzzling it can help prevent problems if you have to do something that may be pain-ful. Never punish a dog for this type of aggression!

Fear

The source of anxious behaviour can often be traced to the first weeks of a dog's life. A shortage of new experiences during the important socialisation phase has great influence on its later behavi-our. A dog that never encountered humans, other dogs or animals during this period will be afraid of them later. This fear is common in dogs brought up in a barn or kennel, with almost no contact with humans. As we saw, fear can lead to aggressive behaviour.

So it's important that a puppy gets as many new impressions as possible in the first weeks of its life. Take it with you into town in the car or on the bus, walk with it down busy streets and allow it to have plenty of contact with humans, other dogs and other animals.

It's a huge task to turn an anxious, poorly socialised dog into a rounded pet. It will probably take a lot of attention, love, patience and energy to get this animal used to everything around it. Reward it often and give it plenty of time to adapt and, over time, it will learn to trust you and become less anxious. Try not to force anything, because this will always have the reverse effect. Here too, an obedience course can help a lot. A dog can be especially afraid of strangers. Let visitors give it something tasty as a treat. Put a can of dog biscuits by the door so that your visitors can spoil your dog when they arrive. Here again, don't try to force anything. If the dog is still frightened, leave it in peace. Dogs are often frightened in certain situations, well-known examples are thunderstorms and fireworks. In these cases try to ignore their anxious behaviour. If

you react to their whimpering and whining, it's the same as rewarding it. If you ignore its fear completely, the dog will quickly learn that nothing is wrong. You can speed up this 'learning process' by rewarding its positive behaviour.

Rewarding

Rewarding forms the basis for bringing up a dog. Rewarding good behaviour works far better than punishing bad behaviour and rewarding is also more fun than punishment. Over time the opinions on upbringing for dogs have gradually changed. In the past the proper way to correct bad behaviour was a sharp pull on the lead. Today, experts view rewarding as a positive incentive to get dogs to do what we expect of them. There are many ways to reward a dog. The usual ways are a stroke or a friendly word, even without a tasty treat to go with it. Of course, a piece of dog biscuit does wonders

when you're training a puppy. Be sure you always have something delicious in your pocket to reward good behaviour. Another form of reward is play. Whenever a dog notices you have a ball in your pocket, it won't go far from your side. As soon as you've finished playing, put the ball away. This way your dog will always do its best in exchange for a game.

Despite the emphasis you put on rewarding good behaviour, a dog can sometimes be a nuisance or disobedient. You must correct such behaviour immediately. Always be consistent: 'no' must always be 'no'.

Barking

Dogs which bark too much and too often are a nuisance for their surroundings. A dog-owner may tolerate barking up to a point, but neighbours are annoyed by the unnecessary noise. Don't encourage your puppy to bark and yelp. Of course, it should be able to announce its presence, but if it goes on barking it must be called to order with a strict 'Quiet!'. If a puppy fails to obey, just hold its muzzle closed with your hand.

A dog will sometimes bark for long periods when left alone. It feels threatened and tries to get someone's attention by barking. There are special training programmes for this problem, where dogs learn that being alone is nothing to be afraid of, and that its master will always return.

You can practice this with your dog at home. Leave the room and come back in at once. Reward your dog if it stays quiet. Gradually increase the length of your absences and keep rewarding it as long as it remains quiet.

Never punish the dog if it does bark or yelp. It will never understand punishment afterwards, and this will only make the problem worse. Never go back into the room as long as your dog is barking, as it will view this as a reward. You might want to make the dog feel more comfortable by switching the radio on for company during your absence. It will eventually learn that you always come back and the barking will reduce. If you don't get the required result, attend an obedience course or consult a behaviour therapist.

Breeding

Like all animals, dogs must follow their instincts, and reproduction is one of nature's important processes. For people who enjoy breeding dogs this is a positive circumstance.

Those who simply want a cosy companion however miss the regular adventures with bitches on heat and unrestrainable dogs like a toothache. But knowing a little about breeding in dogs will help you to understand why they behave the way they do, and what measures you need to take when this happens. The kennel clubs place strict conditions on animals used for breeding. They must be examined for possible congenital defects. This is the breeder's first obligation, and if you breed a litter and sell the puppies without these checks having been made, you can be held liable by the new owners for any costs arising from any inherited defects. These (veterinary) costs can be enormous! So inform yourself in advance. If your bitch meets the requirements, you can get a list of dogs available for breeding from the kennel club. The dogs on this list have passed the health checks and have possibly also been tested for their working capabilities.

The female in season
Bitches become sexually mature at about eight to twelve months. Then they go into season for the

Liability
Breeding dogs is more than simply 1+1= many. You must never breed with your Border Collie without proper consideration, because it can have unpleasant, even financial, consequences. Under the law, a breeder is liable for the 'quality' of his puppies.

first time. They are on heat for two to three weeks. During the first ten days they discharge little drops of blood and they become steadily more attractive to males. The bitch is fertile during the second half of her season, and will accept a male to mate. The best time for mating is then between the tenth and thirteenth day of her season. A female's first season is often shorter and less severe than those that follow. If you do want to breed with your female you must allow this first (and sometimes the second) season to pass. Most bitches go into season twice per year. If you do plan to breed with your Border in the future, then sterilisation is not an option to prevent unwanted offspring. A temporary solution is a contraceptive injection, although this is controversial because of possible side effects such as womb infections.

Phantom pregnancy

A phantom pregnancy is a not uncommon occurrence. The female behaves as if she has a litter. She takes all kinds of things to her basket and treats them like puppies. Her milk teats swell and sometimes milk is actually produced. The female will sometimes behave aggressively towards humans or other animals, as if she is defending her young. Phantom pregnancies usually begin two months after a season and can last a number of weeks. If it happens

to a bitch once, it will often then occur after every season. If she suffers under it, sterilisation is the best solution, because continual phantom pregnancies increase the risk of womb or milk teat conditions. In the short term a hormone treatment is worth trying, also perhaps giving the animal homeopathic medicines. Camphor spirit can give relief when teats are heavily swollen, but rubbing the teats with ice or a cold cloth (moisten and freeze) can also help relieve the pain. Feed the female less than usual, and makes sure she gets enough attention and extra exercise.

Preparing to breed

If you do plan to breed a litter of puppies, you must first wait for your female to be physically and mentally full-grown. In any event you must let her first season pass. As early as possible, some time before the bitch is expected to go in season, start the search for a potential mate. If your female is registered and has passed all the health checks (see the chapter Your Border Collie's health), the kennel club will help to find a suitable dog. If you plan to mate your bitch with a dog not on the kennel club list, think about the following. Do not pick a dog without a pedigree. Convince yourself that he doesn't display any congenital defects. Don't be to concerned about his appearance as it's the grandparents on each side that actually influence the appea-

rance of the pups, and because there are so many varieties of Border Collie they may have been a completely different type. Observe the dog's character and temperament and look for characteristics that will reinforce the positive qualities of your bitch, compensate for any of her weak points or defective personality traits. Never breed two extremes together. If both parents are hyperactive, for example, there's a high chance that this (undesirable) trait will be even stronger in their offspring.

The owner of the dog will expect a certain amount as a cover fee. Sometimes a pup from the future litter may be the fee. Before mating your bitch, check that she's free of any parasites (external and internal). She must be fit, not overweight and vaccinated against all the usual diseases. If you want strong, healthy puppies, the mother-to-be must be in optimum condition. As soon as the female shows the first signs of being on heat, make an appointment with the owner of the male for the first mating attempt. In most cases, after the first apparently successful attempt at mating, the bitch is brought to the dog again after two or three days.

Pregnancy

It's often difficult to tell at first when a bitch is pregnant. Only after about four weeks can you feel the pups in her womb. She will now slowly get fatter and her behaviour will usually change. Her teats will swell during the last few weeks of pregnancy. The average pregnancy lasts 63 days, and costs the bitch more and more energy. In the beginning she is fed her normal amount of food, but her nutritional needs increase in jumps during the second half of the pregnancy. Give her approximately fifteen percent more food each week from the fifth week on. The mother-to-be needs extra energy and proteins during this phase. During the last weeks you can give her a concentrated food, rich in energy, such as dry puppy food. Divide this into several small portions per day, because the growing womb leaves less space for the stomach. At the end of the pregnancy her energy needs can easily be one-and-a-half times more than usual. From about the sixth week, gradually increase her protein intake with more meat, (boiled) eggs, fish and milk in her food. This promotes strong growth of the puppies and keeps the mother in good condition without her gaining too much weight. After about seven weeks the mother will demonstrate nesting behaviour and begin to look for a place to give birth to her young. This might be her own basket or a special birthing box. This must be ready at least a week before the birth to give the mother time to get used to it. The basket or box should preferably be in a quiet place.

The birth

The average litter is between three and nine puppies. The birth usually passes without problems. Border Collie bitches are excellent mothers and usually know what to do instinctively, even with their first litter, so complications during the birth are rare. Of course, you should be in the area during the whole process and the mother will feel more relaxed due to your presence. Intervention is rarely needed but, of course, contact your vet immediately if you suspect a problem!

Suckling

After birth, the mother starts to produce milk. The suckling period is very demanding. During the first three to four weeks the pups rely entirely on their mother's milk. During this time she needs extra food and fluids. This can be up to three or four times the normal amount. If she's producing too little milk, you can give both

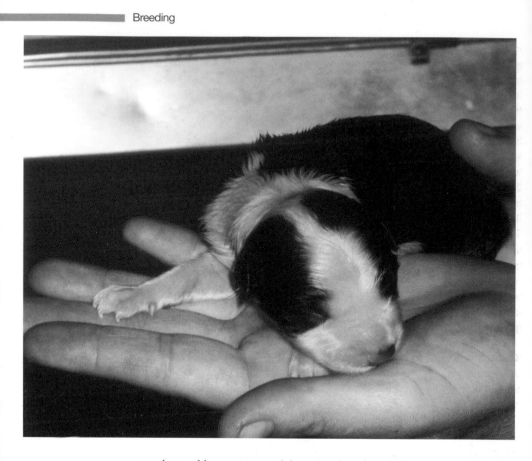

mother and her young special puppy milk. Here too, divide the high quantity of food the mother needs over several smaller portions. Again, choose a concentrated, high-energy, food and give her plenty of fresh drinking water, but not cows milk, which can cause diarrhoea. You can start to feed the pups extra food from the third week. Start with a mush of a soft corn meal (Brinta or Bambix). During the fourth week you can move on to canned puppy food mixed with some brown bread. Puppies are crazy about it and will soon start scrapping to get at their food, so make sure each pup gets its fair share. If you feel that one pup is missing out, set it apart when feeding but do this only as long as necessary and get it eating with its brothers and sisters as quickly as possible. Only that way will it learn to fend for itself. Over-eating is just as dangerous as under-eating, so increase the amount gradually. Watch for the growth and behaviour of the pups and regularly check that their droppings are properly formed. Small hard droppings can be a sign of malnutrition or lack of fluids. Droppings that are too soft or runny are often caused by overfeeding. Between the fifth and sixth week, you can switch to a puppy meal, perhaps with a little water added at the beginning. Ideally, the puppies are now fully weaned off, i.e. they no longer drink their mother's milk. The mother's milk production gradually stops and her food needs also drop. Within a couple of weeks after weaning, the mother should again be getting the same amount of food as before the pregnancy.

Castration and sterilisation

As soon as you are sure your bitch should never bear a (new) litter, a vasectomy or sterilisation is the best solution. During sterilisation, the uterus, and often the womb, is surgically removed (in fact this is actually castration). The bitch no longer goes into season and can never become pregnant. The best age for a sterilisation is about eighteen months, when the bitch is more or less fully-grown.

A male dog is usually only castrated for medical reasons or to correct undesirable sexual behaviour. During a castration the testicles are removed, which is a simple procedure and usually without complications. There is no special age for castration. Where possible, wait until the dog is fully-grown. Vasectomy is sufficient where it's only a case of making the dog infertile. In this case the dog keeps its sexual drive but can no longer reproduce.

Shows and sport

The Border Collie is a real working dog that is not born for an easy life. It will become a companion at home, but only as long as you spend enough time with it.

They love to work with sheep or other animals and this is the life they're born to. If you can't give them that work, then you have to find alternatives. Your Border is bursting with energy and probably has many hidden talents. Choosing a Border Collie as a companion needs serious consideration, and means that you are prepared to meet its physical and psychological needs. If you plan to participate in dog shows with your Border, you have to realise that such an activity can be of no more than subordinate importance for this dog.

Exhibitions and exemption shows

Visiting a dog show is a pleasant experience for both dog and master, and for some dog-lovers is an intensive hobby. They visit

countless shows every year. Others find it nice to visit an exemption show with their dog just once. It's worth making the effort to visit an exemption show where a judge's experienced eyes will inspect your Border Collie and assess it for form, gait, condition and behaviour. The judge's report will teach you your dog's weak and strong points, which may help you when choosing a mate for breeding. You can also exchange experiences with other owners of the breed. Official exemption shows are only open to dogs with a pedigree.

Ring training

If you've never been to an exemption show with your dog, you're probably unaware of what will be expected of you and your dog. Many kennel clubs organise so-called ring training courses for dogs going to an exemption show for the first time. This training teaches you exactly what the judge will be looking for, and you can practice this together with your dog.

Club matches

Almost all kennel clubs organise club matches. You must register your dog in advance in a certain class. These meetings are usually small and friendly and are often the first acquaintance dog and master make with a judge. This is an overwhelming experience for your dog; a lot of its contemporaries and a strange man or woman who fiddles around with it and peers into its mouth. After a few

moments, your dog will know exactly what's expected of it and will happily go to the next club match.

Championship shows

Various championship shows take place during the course of the year with different prizes. Your dog must be registered in a certain class in advance and it will then be listed in a catalogue. On the day itself the dog is kept in a cage until its turn comes up. During the judging in the ring, it's important that you show your dog at its best. The judge gives an official judgement and makes a report. When all the dogs from that class have been judged, the best are selected. After the judging for that breed is

finished, you can pick up your report and any prize you may have won. The winners of the various classes then compete for the title Best of Breed where a winner is chosen from all the dogs in the same breed group. Finally, the winners of each breed group compete for the title of Best in Show. Of course, your dog must look very smart for the show. The judge will not be impressed if its coat is not clean or is tangled and its paws are dirty. Nails must be clipped and teeth free of plaque. The dog must also be free of parasites and ailments. A bitch must not be in season and a male must be in possession of both testicles. Apart from those things, judges also hate badly brought-up, anxious or nervous dogs.

Sport

Sheepdog trials

Even if you're not in a position to give your Border Collie work to do every day, because you don't have sheep or other animals, you can still let your dog develop its original skills. There are various training centres where experienced trainers will help you work on the in-born working characteristics of your Border. You can probably give it no greater pleasure; herding and driving animals is simply in its blood.

More and more people are discovering sheep driving as a sport and quickly learn how addictive it is. Once the dog has mastered the most important manoeuvres and is sufficiently under control, you can

compete in sheepdog trials. These events judge the dog's working capabilities in practical circumstances and in a competitive environment. The dog must respond to the handler's (its master's) instructions given in verbal and/or whistle commands and herd a flock of sheep over a set course. This course consists of a number of fixed elements: the Outrun (to get control of a flock of sheep that has been set some 400 metres away by running wide curves left and right behind them); the Lift, getting the sheep moving in a controlled fashion, followed by the Fetch, bringing the flock (in a straight line) to the handler (its master). Then the dog has to drive the sheep around a triangular course (the Drive), including driving them through a pair of gates. Finally a pair of sheep are set apart from the flock (the Shed), after which the whole flock has to be driven into a small fenced area

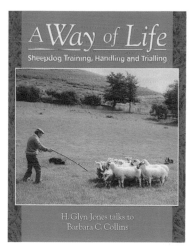

A Way of Life : Sheepdog training, handling and trialling by International Supreme Champion H Glyn Jones and Barbara Collins. Hardback, 192 pages inc.125 illustrations. Published 1987. ISBN 1-903366-27-5

(the Pen). The whole course must be completed within a set time limit, usually twelve minutes. A maximum number of points is set for each component. Subtraction of points for mistakes gives the final score for dog and handler.

Obedience
You can follow up on basic obedience training by trying to win

the Behaviour and Obedience diplomas, classes 1, 2 & 3, with increasing degrees of difficulty. This discipline is also practised in a competitive environment, and there are British, European and World Championships. Among other things the dog must walk on the lead, follow at foot off the lead, stay standing or sit or lie for a set time while its master walks away and is out of sight for several minutes. Tracking and retrieving is trained and tested almost to perfection.

The British form of Obedience goes a step further, the accent here is on perfect performance of the tasks set. Highly intensive training is intended to make dog and master one unit which during the performance of several exercises seems to be glued together. Obedience is only practised in competition, there are no diplomas.

Agility

The Border Collie excels in this popular sport too. The combination of master and dog must

Agility

Flyballlauncher

cover a set course with countless obstacles as fast and with as few faults as possible. This sport is demanding on both dog and master and requires that they are both very fit. The dog must be able to perform both high and long jumps and come to terms with obstacles such as a tunnel, a gangway, slalom poles and a series of devices (fence, catwalk and seesaw).

Then it has to catch the ball cleanly and run back along the same course as fast as possible to bring it to its master.

Flyball

Flyball originated in America and is becoming ever more popular. It is played by two teams of four dogs each. Each dog has to jump over four obstacles to get to a machine that shoots balls and then activate the machine by pressing on a small plan with its paws.

Flyballhurdle

Parasites

All dogs are vulnerable to various sorts of parasite. Parasites are tiny creatures that live at the expense of another animal. They feed on blood, skin and other body substances.

There are two main types. Internal parasites live within their host animal's body (tapeworm and round-worm) and external parasites live on the animals exterior, usually in its coat (fleas and ticks), but also in its ears (ear mite).

Fleas

Fleas feed on a dog's blood. They cause not only itching and skin problems, but can also carry infections such as tapeworm. In large numbers they can cause anaemia and dogs can also become allergic to a flea's saliva, which can cause serious skin conditions. So it's important to treat dog for fleas as effectively as possible, not just on the dog itself but also in its surroundings. For treatment on the animal, there are various medicines: drops for the neck and to put it in its food, flea collars, long-life sprays and flea powders. There are various sprays in pet shops that can be used to eradicate fleas in the dog's immediate surroundings. Choose a spray that kills both adult fleas and their larvae. If your dog goes in your car, you should spray that too. Fleas can also affect other pets, so you should treat those too. When spraying a room, cover any aquariums or fishbowls. If the spray reaches the water, it can be fatal for your fish! Your vet and pet shop have a wide range of flea treatments and can advise you.

Ticks

Ticks are small, spider-like parasites. They feed on the blood of the animal or person they've settled on. A tick looks like a tiny, grey-coloured leather bag with eight feet. When it has sucked itself full, it can easily be five to ten times its own size and is darker in colour. Dogs usually fall victim to tics in bushes, woods or long grass. Ticks cause not only irritation by their blood-sucking, but can also carry a number of serious diseases. This applies especially to the Mediterranean countries, which can be infested with blood parasites. In our country these diseases are fortunately less common. But Lymes disease, which can also affect humans, has reached our shores. Your vet can prescribe a special treatment if you're planning to take your dog to southern Europe. It is important to fight ticks as effectively as possible. Check your dog regularly, especially when it's been running free in woods and bushes. It can also wear an anti-tick collar. Removing a tick is simple using a tick pincette. Grip the tick with the pincette, as close to the dog's skin as possible and carefully pull it out. You can also grip the tick between your fingers and, using a turning movement, pull it carefully out. You must disinfect the spot where the tick had been using iodine to prevent infection. Never soak the tick in alcohol, ether or oil. In a shock reaction the tick may discharge the infected contents of its stomach into the dog's skin.

Worms

Dogs can suffer from various types of worm. The most common are tapeworm and roundworm. Tapeworm causes diarrhoea and poor condition. With a tapeworm infection you can sometimes find small pieces of the worm around the dog's anus or on its bed. In this case, the dog must be wormed. You should also check your dog for fleas, which carry the tapeworm infection. Roundworm is a condition that reoccurs regularly. Puppies are often infected by their mother's milk. Your vet has medicines to prevent this. Roundworm causes problems, particularly in younger dogs, such as diarrhoea, loss of weight and stagnated growth. In serious cases the pup becomes thin, but with a swollen belly. It may vomit and you can then see the worms in its vomit. They are spaghetti-like tendrils. A puppy must be treated for worms every three months during its first year. Adult dogs should be treated every six months.

Tick

Roundworm

Tapeworm

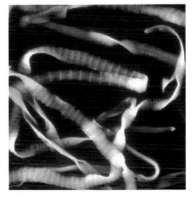

Your Border Collie's health

The space in this book is too limited to go into the medical ups and downs of the Border Collie. But we do want to give some brief information about ailments and disorders that affect this breed more than other dogs.

Typical Border Collie ailments
Dysplasia types
Dysplasia (deviant deformation) can affect all joints. Hip Dysplasia often affects dogs, especially the larger breeds.

Hip Dysplasia (HD)
Hip Dysplasia is an abnormality of the hip joints in the hind quarters, whereby the socket of the hip joint and the head of the upper thigh don't properly match. This causes inflammation and bone tumours, which can be very painful. Until recently, it was assumed that HD was primarily caused by genetic factors. Recent investigations, however, indicate that while genetic factors certainly play a role in terms of a dog's susceptibility to HD, external factors such as food quality and exercise appe-

ar at least equally important. Limit the chance of HD as far as possible by giving your dog ready-made food from a good brand, and don't add any supplements! Make sure your dog doesn't get too fat. A Border Collie pup must certainly be protected from HD in its first year. Don't let him romp too much with other dogs or chase sticks and balls too wildly. These kinds of games cause the pup to make abrupt and risky movements, which can overburden its soft joints. One important but under-estimated factor behind HD is the floor in your home. Parquet and tiled floors are much too slippery for a young dog. Regular slipping can cause complications that promote HD. If you have a smooth floor, it's advisable to lay blankets or old carpet in places the dog uses regularly. Let it spend lots of time in the garden, as grass is a perfect surface to run on.

Elbow Dysplasia (ED)

Elbow Dysplasia generally appears during the first year of a puppy's life. This condition is similar to HD, but affects the forelegs. In the worst case ED can cause lameness. An operation is then needed, which is usually successful. The measures you can take to reduce the chance of ED are the same as for HD.

Progressive Retina Atrophy (PRA)

'Progressive ' means that the condition will steadily worsen and 'Atrophy' means a degenerative condition. The disease is thus a progressive degeneration of the retina that inevitably leads to blindness. PRA is a bothersome condition; once it's found its way into the bloodline, it's difficult to eradicate. In the early stages, the dog will still be able to see well in daylight until it's about five years old. The degeneration process occurs symmetrically in both eyes, is painless but leads to complete blindness between the dog's fifth and tenth year.

Collie Eye Anomaly (CEA)

CEA is equally incurable. The cause is a poorly developed vascular layer (choroid), a membrane that lies behind the retina and supplies it with blood. If the retina doesn't get enough blood the eye can become clouded. CEA is not progressive, meaning the condition won't worsen after birth. But all kinds of complications, such as retinal detachment, can lead to total blindness. Because CEA is non-progressive (the condition is thus usually not noticed), and especially because of the way it is passed on genetically, it represents a serious threat. Only if both parents carry the abnormality will the puppies show the condition. If only one parent suffers from the condition, the pups can become

carriers without actually suffering themselves. So this condition can spread unnoticed and rapidly in a certain population if not checked for, and if all carriers are not prevented from breeding.

Cataracts

Checks for cataracts are made at the same time as the checks for PRA and CEA. This condition causes a clouding of the retina. It can appear in young animals and is passed on by both parents. If only a part of the retina is affected cataracts need not lead to total blindness, but unfortunately this is the consequence in most cases.

Entropion and ectropion

These are genetic conditions affecting the eyelids. With entropion the eyelids are curled inwards, with ectropion outwards. Both cause the eyelashes to lay on the eyeball causing irritation, which leads to red, watering eyes. The eyes become infected and discharge pus. This can cause serious damage to the cornea and eventually even cause blindness. Entropion and ectropion can be corrected surgically.

All Border Collies used for breeding must be checked annually for congenital eye disorders up to their sixth year.

Internet

A great deal of information can be found on the internet. A selection of websites with interesting details and links to other sites and pages is listed here. Sometimes pages move to another site or address. You can find more sites by using the available search-machines.

www.bordercollies.co.uk
This website provides information to help both owner and dog with handling sheep, basic obedience, problem solving and to understand the dog and relate to its way of thinking, plus countless other related topics.

www.bordercollies.com
The one stop source for border collie items.

www.isds.org.uk/index.htm
International sheep dog society.

www.vimick.co.uk
The website of a small breeding kennels near Boston in Lincolnshire.

www.bordercollie.gb.com
A website of Derek Scrimgeour one of the UK's premier sheepdog handlers and trainers. Here you can find more information on sheepdog training and dogs/puppies for sale.

www.bordercollietrustgb.org.uk
The trust is a registered charity which relies on public support to assist Border collies in the UK.

www.bordercollierescue.org
This is the Website of The Border Collie Rescue Society.

www.mastamariner.com home.html
A small but very special English kennel of Border Collies.

www.gis.net/~shepdog/BC_ Museum/index.html
Here you can find two kinds of exhibits that will give you an idea of what kind of dog a Border Collie is and what went into the making of the breed.

Other books from About Pets

Key features of the series are:
- Most affordable books
- Packed with hands-on information
- Well written by experts
- Easy to understand language
- Full colour original photography
- 70 to 110 photos
- All one needs to know to care well for their pet
- Trusted authors, veterinary consultants, breed and species expert authorities
- Appropriate for first time pet owners
- Interesting detailed information for pet professionals
- Title range includes books for advanced pet owners and breeders
- Includes useful addresses, veterinary data, breed standards.

about pets

Breeder clubs

Becoming a member of a breeder club can be very useful for good advice and interesting activities. Contact the Kennel Club in case addresses or telephonenumbers are changed.

The Kennel Club
1 Clarges Street
London UK
W1J 8AB
Tel: 0870 606 6750
Fax: 020 7518 1058
Website: http://www.thekennel
club.org.uk

**The Secretary General
Scottish Kennel Club**
Eskmills Park
Station Road
Musselborough EH21 7PQ
Tel: 0131 665 3920
Fax: 0131 653 6937
www.scottishkennelclub.org
email:info@scottishkennelclub.org

**The Irish Kennel
Club LTD**
Fottrell House, Harold's
Cross Bridge, Dublin 6W.
Ireland.
Telephone (01) 4533300 -
4532309 - 4532310.
Fax (01) 4533237
E-Mail ikenclub@indigo.ie
http://www.ikc.ie/

**Border Collie
Club of GB**
Sec. Mr Collins.
Tel: 0161 718 8415
Website: www.bordercollieclub.com
email: info@bordercollieclub.com

Border Collie Club of Wales

Sec. Mr Clarke.
Tel: 01606 738078

East Anglian Border Collie Club

Secretary Mrs Christina Dalby
Tel: 01707 338657
Email : axernamoon@btopen-world.com

Midlands Border Collie Club

Secretary
Lyn Norton
49 Snowshill Close
Church Hill North
Redditch
Worcs
Tel: 01527 595820
Fax : 01527 595820
Email :
mbcc.info@blueyonder.co.uk

North West Border Collie Club

Sec. Mrs Richardson.
Tel: 0161 703 8395

Scottish Border Collie Club

Sec. Ms C Park.
Tel: Not available -
for more information contact
The Kennel Club Website:
http://www.champdogs.co.uk

Southern Border Collie Club

Sec. Mrs S M Wittington.
Tel: 01622 813529

West of England Border Collie Club

Sec. Mrs Hanlon
Tel: 01380 724740 Secretary
Prue Griffiths
Email :
K9Photos@compuserve.com

The Border Collie

Origin:	Great Britain
FCI-classification:	Group I: Sheepdogs and cattle dogs
First breed standard:	1976
Original use:	Sheepdog
Use today:	Sheepdog, tracker and blind-dog, sporting dog
Shoulder height:	Males 53 cm, bitches slightly smaller
Weight:	15 - 20 kg
Life expectancy (average):	12 - 15 years

the **Border Collie**